ALL ABOUT TEETH

by Nicole A. Mansfield

PEBBLE
a capstone imprint

Published by Pebble, an imprint of Capstone
1710 Roe Crest Drive, North Mankato, Minnesota 56003
capstonepub.com

Copyright © 2023 by Capstone. All rights reserved. No part of this publication may be reproduced in whole or in part, or stored in a retrieval system, or transmitted in any form or by any means, electronic, mechanical, photocopying, recording, or otherwise, without written permission of the publisher.

Library of Congress Cataloging-in-Publication Data
Names: Mansfield, Nicole A., author.
Title: All about teeth / by Nicole A. Mansfield.
Description: North Mankato, Minnesota : Pebble, an imprint of Capstone, [2023] | Series: My teeth | Includes bibliographical references and index. | Audience: Ages 5–8 | Audience: Grades K–1 | Summary: "Smile big and take a good look at your teeth. How much do they really do? What are they made of? And why do they fall out? Find out in this easy-to-read Pebble Emerge book. With simple text and color photos, young readers will learn all about their teeth"— Provided by publisher.
Identifiers: LCCN 2022024824 (print) | LCCN 2022024825 (ebook) |
    ISBN 9780756570811 (hardcover) | ISBN 9780756571009 (paperback) |
    ISBN 9780756570903 (ebook PDF) | ISBN 9780756571023 (kindle edition)
Subjects: LCSH: Teeth—Juvenile literature.
Classification: LCC QP88.6 .M36 2023 (print) | LCC QP88.6 (ebook) | DDC 612.3/11—dc23/eng/20220614
    LC record available at https://lccn.loc.gov/2022024824
    LC ebook record available at https://lccn.loc.gov/2022024825

Editorial Credits
Editor: Ericka Smith; Designer: Sarah Bennett; Media Researcher: Svetlana Zhurkin; Production Specialist: Katy LaVigne

Consultant Credits
Patricia V. Hermanson, DMD, MS

Image Credits
Getty Images: Don Mason, 18, Jose Luis Pelaez Inc, 19, Subir Basak, 15, Westend61, 14; Shutterstock: Andriyana Dadan, cover (design elements), Annette Shaff, 5, cigdem, 10, Designifty, 1 (smiling tooth), Dusitara Stocker, 13, EvgeniiAnd, 17, Maxx-Studio, 7, 9, Monkey Business Images, 4, Noey smiley, 11, Perfectorius, cover (design elements), Rvector (background), 3, 22–23, 24, Take A Pix Media, cover, Tetyana Kaganska, 6, wavebreakmedia, 12, Zhanna Markina (background), cover, back cover, and throughout; Svetlana Zhurkin: 20, 21

All internet sites appearing in back matter were available and accurate when this book was sent to press.

Table of Contents

What Do You Know About Teeth? 4

Take a Tooth Tour! 6

How Teeth Grow 12

What Is a Tooth's Job? 16

    Tasty, Toothy Treat 20

    Glossary 22

    Read More 23

    Internet Sites 23

    Index 24

    About the Author 24

Words in **bold** are in the glossary.

What Do You Know About Teeth?

Did you know that most kids your age have 20 teeth? That's 12 less than an adult has!

You can count your teeth. Move your tongue from tooth to tooth inside your mouth. Count each one!

Take a Tooth Tour!

Teeth are an important part of your body. They are made up of four layers. Each layer has a job to do.

The outside layer is called **enamel**. It helps protect your teeth from **decay**. Enamel is strong. It's stronger than your bones!

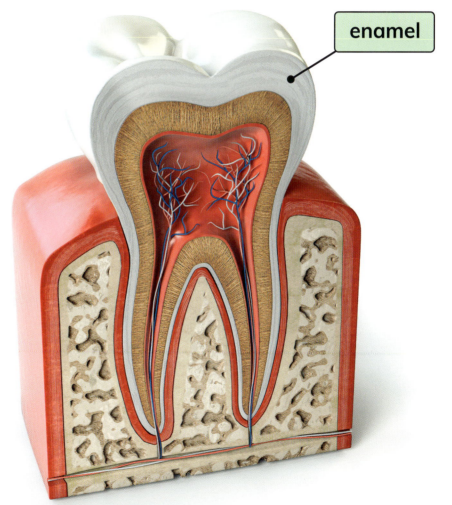

The next layer is **dentin**. It helps support the enamel. It's made of tiny tubes! Dentin is hard too, but not as hard as enamel.

The third layer is called **cementum**. It surrounds a tooth's root. The root is the part of your tooth below your **gums**. It connects your tooth to your jaw bone.

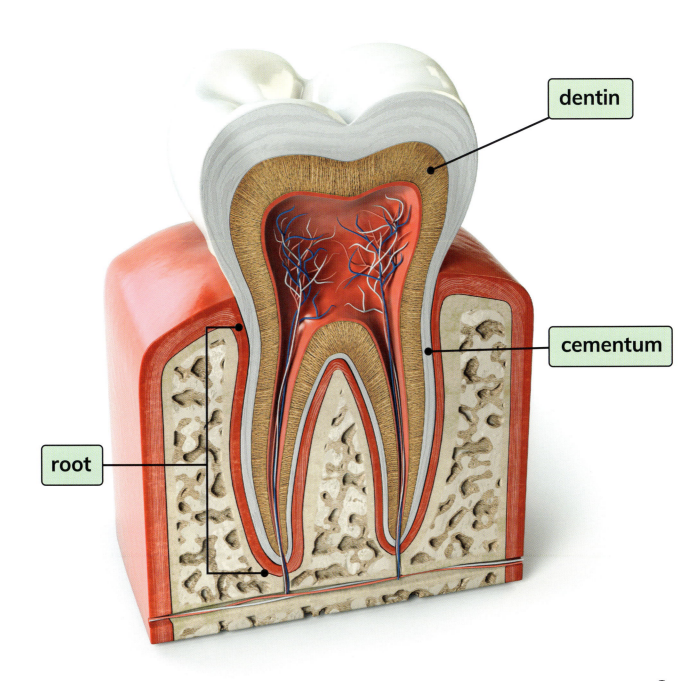

Pulp is the last layer. It is on the inside of a tooth. Pulp is soft. It is very **sensitive**. It must always be protected by the other layers of your tooth.

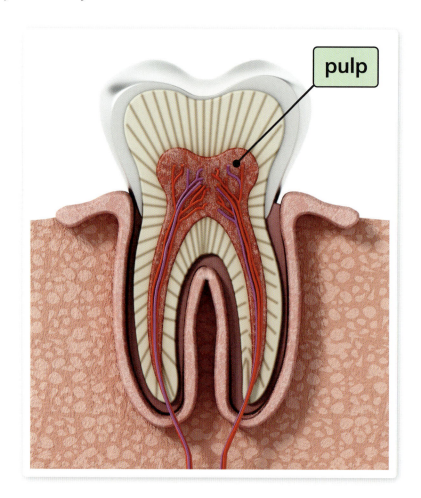

The pulp's job is to send messages from your teeth to your brain. It tells your brain when something is too hot or cold. It can also tell your brain that something hurts.

How Teeth Grow

Babies are born without teeth showing. They don't need teeth. They only drink milk at first.

But hidden under a baby's gums are plenty of teeth. They're just waiting to push through the gums! When a baby is about six months old, their first tooth starts to grow in.

Kids have 20 teeth. They have 10 teeth on the top and 10 teeth on the bottom. These teeth are small.

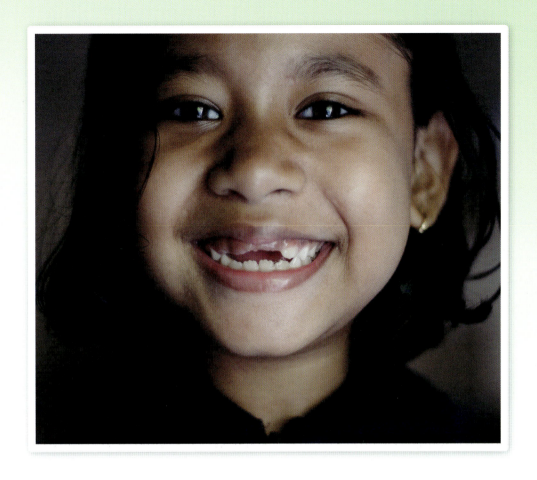

As kids grow, so do their heads and jaws. In a few years, their baby teeth will start to fall out. This makes room for the bigger adult teeth to grow in.

What Is a Tooth's Job?

Chewing food is one of our teeth's biggest jobs. Different teeth do different things. Some teeth tear food. Some teeth smash up food so that we can swallow it.

Some people think that teeth are just for chewing food. But that's not all they do. Teeth have a few jobs every day.

Teeth help us speak. They control the air moving out of our mouths. That helps us **pronounce** words. Teeth also help us smile. Our smiles help show our feelings.

Teeth do many important things! So take good care of them. Brush and floss them every day. And visit your dentist for regular checkups.

Tasty, Toothy Treat

This treat is healthy and fun. It will put a smile on your face once you try it! Ask a caregiver to help you.

If you have nut allergies, ask your caregiver to help you think of something tasty—like cream cheese—to use instead of nut butter.

What You Need

- a spoon or butter knife
- 4 tablespoons of any nut butter
- 1 apple (with the core removed and sliced into eight pieces)
- 20 miniature marshmallows

What You Do

1. Use the spoon or butter knife to spread about ½ tablespoon of nut butter on one side of all eight apple slices.

2. Place five miniature marshmallows in a row on top of four of the apple slices.

3. Place an apple slice with no marshmallows, nut butter side down, on top of each of the four apple slices with marshmallows.

You've made a tasty, toothy smile. Share your snack with your friends and family. And be sure to brush your teeth after your snack!

Glossary

cementum (sih-MEN-tuhm)—the outer surface of the root of a tooth

decay (di-KAY)—breaking down

dentin (DEN-tin)—the layer of a tooth that surrounds the tooth's pulp

enamel (ih-NAM-uhl)—the hard outer surface of a tooth

gum (GUHM)—the firm flesh around the base of a person's tooth

pronounce (pro-NOWNSS)—to say the correct way

pulp (PUHLP)—the soft, sensitive part of a tooth

sensitive (sen-SIH-tiv)—easily damaged

Read More

Jenkins, Pete. *Teeth.* Vero Beach, FL: Rourke Educational Media, 2017.

Mansfield, Nicole A. *Keeping Your Teeth Clean.* North Mankato, MN: Capstone, 2023.

Schuh, Mari. *Caring for Your Teeth.* North Mankato, MN: Capstone, 2022.

Internet Sites

Britannica Kids: Teeth
kids.britannica.com/kids/article/teeth/353840

KidsHealth: Mouth and Teeth
kidshealth.org/en/parents/mouth-teeth.html

YouTube: Teeth: Not Just for Smiles!
youtube.com/watch?v=b5CPd1_r03s

Index

adult teeth, 15

baby teeth, 13–15

cementum, 8

decay, 7

dentin, 8

enamel, 7, 8

gums, 8, 13

pulp, 10–11

roots, 8

About the Author

Nicole A. Mansfield dedicates all of her children's books to her own three children—Victorious, Justine, and Zion. She lives in Georgia and is passionate about singing at her church. Nicole loves to take long walks with her kids and her active-duty military husband of 19 years.